The Sabbath Bee
Love Songs to Shabbat

Wilhelmina Gottschalk

Ben Yehuda Press
Teaneck, New Jersey

THE SABBATH BEE. Copyright ©2018 by Wilhelmina Gottschalk. All rights reserved. No part of this book may be used or reproduced in any manner whatsoever without written permission except in the case of brief quotations embodied in critical articles and reviews.

Published by Ben Yehuda Press
122 Ayers Court #1B
Teaneck, NJ 07666
http://www.BenYehudaPress.com

ISBN13: 978-1-934730-69-0

Cover illustration by Katie Skau

18 19 20 / 5 4 3 2 1

܀

This book made possible
through the generosity of
Judy Heicklen

Dedicated to my husband
Rabbi Neil Schuman
Who brought poetry to my life of prose

܀

Contents

Introduction	vii
The day after Purim	1
Candle afterglow	2
Running over	3
Brought forth	4
The Muse-Shabbat smackdown	5
The first real day of spring	6
Geode	7
Kneading	8
The Sabbath bee	9
No briefcase	10
Dancing shoes	11
Pet shop with allegory	12
Double manna	13
Big and small	14
Invisible royalty	15
Clubhouse	16
Blind date	17
Just be	18
Grandpa's house	19
Creeping sunlight	20
Four somethings	21
Came for me	22
Blanket	23
Closets	24
To the Choirmaster: A solo for violin	25
Storm	26
The bride	27
Letter	28
The luckiest person	29
Water damage	30
Beads	31
Combat nurse	32
Not white	33
Nothing new	34
The sleepy guest	35
Becomes easy	36
Looked everywhere	37

Just cuddle	38
Time change	39
Guerilla performance art	40
Nights like this	41
Winter wonderland	42
Stopping by the bookstore on a snowy evening	43
Pockets of delight	44
Holiday guests	45
Winter white	46
Tropical paradise	47
The cover of night	48
Snowflakes	49
In a single word	50
Fairy tale	51
On Shabbat	52
Pity date	53
Above the tablecloth	54
Sunday's child	55
Cause and effect	56
The Sabbath tree	57
Haiku	58
Lifeblood	59
Hiddur mitzvah	60
Flower bride	61
Exact timing	62
Macaroni necklace	63
Pomegranate	64
Wardrobe choice	65
Quiet spaces	66
The art of a perfect sunset	67
A song for Shabbat	68
Road ends	69
Reluctant Shabbat	70
Stayed the night	71
Memory lane	72
Weekday ruins	73
Too far	74
Havdalah	75
Water balloons	76

Introduction

The earliest glimmers of *The Sabbath Bee* came into being shortly after the holidays in 2007, on *Shabbat Noach*. I later dubbed the day *Shabbat Normal* because it was our first return to the regular weekly rhythm after a month of joyful, soul-searching, thought-provoking and sometimes uncomfortable holiday upsets.

The timing is significant because, due to that year's series of three-day holidays and Yom Kippur's invasion of Shabbat, we had gone for a solid month without offering a single welcoming party for the Sabbath bride. It was as if she had come in quietly through the service entrance week after week, ceding her position to the visiting dignitaries of the month of Tishrei.

I didn't realize how much I had missed her grand entry until the evening of *Shabbat Normal*, when we began to sing. Though I cannot be certain that the collective spirit in the room was higher than usual on that night, I felt that everyone around me was just as enthusiastic as I was about *finally* bringing Shabbat back to her place of honor. We welcomed the Sabbath bride not like a weekly visitor but as a long-awaited, yearned-for beloved.

During *L'kah Dodi*, as we sang about the arrival of Shabbat in the words of Judaism's mystic tradition, I felt that Shabbat herself was sharing our eagerness for a true reunion. Excitement drummed through me while voices thundered similar sentiments and words of welcome from all sides. The whole community seemed to be saying, person by person, "*Finally*, it can be just me and you again—with no distractions." When we turned to the door to greet Shabbat, she entered as if on New Year's Eve—with champagne, confetti and a breath-hitching kiss.

That evening's reunion gave me a more intimate appreciation of Shabbat than any that I had experienced before, demonstrating what the Kabbalists meant by "the bride" and "the queen."

Without meaning to at first, I began to image Shabbat in various guises, making a unique entrance every week. I kept these images to myself for about half a year, until a bleary-eyed post-Purim Shabbat demanded that I share it. The positive responses I received led me to begin recording the outcomes of my encounters with Shabbat week by week.

The Sabbath Bee is the outcome of this experience, of a game that I play with Shabbat. It is midrash—a living reinterpretation, a story designed to bring new ideas into an ancient institution and apply fresh understandings to a heavily examined religious structure.

For those familiar with the mystical side of Judaism or the Friday night liturgy, there's nothing unusual about referring to Shabbat as a bride or queen. The white dress and the crown require a sizeable mental leap, since in our everyday comparisons of this-to-that, we rarely go so far as to compare days to people. I would probably get weird reactions if I tried telling a friend that he was like a breath of Thursday, and most personifications of days of the week invariably end with clichéd images—Monday with his briefcase, Sunday reading the paper during a leisurely breakfast.

In Shabbat's case, the talk of brides and queens is all about big, transcendent emotional connections. Shabbat demands certain behaviors, and the Jewish people scramble to obey these commands. We are married to Shabbat because we've sworn an oath of loyalty to this day—with all of the grandeur and restrictions that a lifelong contract should entail. Every week is an opportunity to prepare a celebratory feast, to await sunset with the joy and jumping-up-and-down excitement of a groom about to meet his bride.

However, images of brides and queens can only tell some of the story. Some facts that are true of Shabbat are not true of a bride. There are times when Shabbat might be more like a visiting uncle than a queen. And for that matter, as a citizen of a representative democracy, how should I feel about royalty? By calling Shabbat a queen, am I saying that it is respected, powerful and compassionate or am I calling it an impotent a symbol of an outdated system?

Also, I sometimes prefer to drop the bride imagery for something a little more heterosexual. Sometimes. Femininity is so deeply ingrained into Shabbat that it often feels… wrong… to give this day a Y chromosome. Still, if Shabbat can be a queen, doesn't it stand to reason that he can also be a grandparent? Or a blanket? Or, to take an idea from the Kabbalist Shlomo Halevi, the ruins of a mighty city? How about a jealous girlfriend that sabotages your relationships with other people? There are definitely times in my life when Shabbat is the jealous girlfriend.

That brings up another reason why I put together *The Sabbath Bee*. Shabbat is different every week, because we are different every week. Sometimes Shabbat shows up with dancing shoes, other weeks with a cup of cocoa and a bedtime story. Whether or not it *should* be, Shabbat cannot be a wedding banquet every single week of the year. Sometimes the table is set with fine china and a dozen cheerful guests are at the door, while other nights a quick shower and a sandwich are all I can manage before sunset. One week I might say, "*Oh*, it's Friday again!" and the next, "Oh. It's Friday. *Again?*" Shabbat can evoke both emotions, and everything in between.

Therefore, each week I let Shabbat come as it will. Some weeks Shabbat might be happy to give me a quick hug and let me return to my conversation with friends, while other nights the prospect of a mystical joining is so exhilarating that Shabbat and I sneak away together to the nearest janitor's closet.

I hope that some of the vignettes will resonate with you, and maybe even help to expand your own ideas and feelings about Shabbat. Some of the passages, I know, will be meaningless or even off-putting to some. A living tradition inhales and exhales, and concepts that are greater than human endeavor cannot be fully described by any single finite comparison—or even a cacophony of them. Still, hundreds of thousands of facets all taken together might form a reasonable outline of ineffable perfection.

The Sabbath Bee

The day after Purim

Shabbat arrives as usual, dressed in silk with her hair and make-up beautifully arranged.

The room is a mess, and with the exception of a pair of candles glowing on the table it seems that nothing has been prepared.

"What is this?" Shabbat demands. "You knew I was coming! Where is my welcome?"

I scramble, bleary-eyed, to a seated position on the couch. "I'm sorry—really sorry Shabbat, but last night your little brother came in from Persia. He kept me up *all night* partying. Then this morning he pulls me out of bed *again*, just a few hours after I fell asleep. He's exhausting!"

"Oh, him." Shabbat settles beside me on the couch. "Did the two of you have a good time, at least?"

"He's a fabulous guy." I lean into her, nuzzling her neck. "But I'm glad you're here now."

Candle afterglow

When the candle wicks start to burn, it's easy to see the world in a different light. There's a subtle sheen that influences vision as soon as she lights the candles, making colors brighter and surfaces shinier.

It creeps into the children's room and makes the ponies and dinosaurs on the glossy covers rear and dance. It smooths over photographs and makes the subjects younger, happier than they were even in the glow of the camera flash. It's a light that brings twinkles to eyes and illumines the darkest corners—at least for a few moments.

It does sputter and fade before true dark sets in, of course. It's not for keeping—just for enjoying.

Running over

Shabbat remains bottled all week, shelved and corked, but present. On Friday night it is unstopped and released into the world, filling every cup in the house and spilling over the table's edge.

Shabbat continues pouring out, drenching my fingers and seeping into my shoes. Soon the entire house will be ankle-deep in Shabbat.

After the front door crashes open, Shabbat continues to pour out into the world.

Brought forth

The last of the weekday grunge is wiped clean, so that you are empty and waiting.

The first sweetness and warmth of Shabbat feed your rising song, and each psalm brings a new ingredient. You dance back and forth, mixing together into a pliable mass that folds in on itself, kneading in and out with the pace of a heartbeat. Emotions press softly outward, voices weave together in a mindfully prepared and delicious symphony.

And in the end, if there is fire in your prayers, you will create something that can sustain you.

The Muse-Shabbat smackdown

Friday at 6:45, my muse knocks on the door.

Shabbat answers. "Oh, it's you. What do *you* want?" she asks.

"Who is it?" I call.

My muse starts to answer, but Shabbat cuts her off. "No one! Just a salesperson!" She glares at my muse. "You can't come in now. It's *my* time."

My muse raises her hands in confusion, diaphanous robes fluttering. "But, I just have this one really great idea—"

"Tough. Come back in twenty-five hours."

"Can I just leave a message? A short little—"

Shabbat glares. "I don't take dictation," she says, slamming the door in my muse's face.

I watch from the end of the hallway, slipping back into the kitchen before Shabbat turns around. When she glides back into the room and cups her body against my back, I pretend nothing happened.

Shabbat is a taste of paradise, but she can be jealous.

The first real day of spring:
ימין ושמאל תפרוצי

After six months of winter, Shabbat exploded into spring. To the left and to the right, daffodils and apple blossoms, fresh grass and blushes of green burst out. Shabbat brought with it the first perfect day of spring.

…Except that it wasn't the first. Thursday was just as nice. Thursday was just as warm. But on Thursday, sunrise to sunset, I had ten minutes to spend outside.

Shabbat is not a perfect day. Shabbat is not the warm breeze, the fresh air or the greening terrain. These things could appear any day of the week.

So, what is Shabbat? Shabbat is the walk in the park, the moment spent under the apple tree. Shabbat is the chance to taste the sweetness that languished, unappreciated, for the first six days of the week.

Geode

Shabbat is a time for contracting, for drawing in the widespread arms and fingers of influence. It is a time to abdicate some of the enormous responsibility of the earth, to admit that the sun and moon will continue dancing across the sky whether or not we try to prod them on their way.

On Shabbat, the world becomes a geode. It sits and waits. Later, when we look into it, we might find just a few tattered shards of meaning. On a perfect, transcendent week though, the simple act of drawing back from mundane concerns might lead to something entirely new—a glittering paradise that would never have been possible in a more densely packed world.

Kneading

Dear SK—
I don't go to this much trouble for most people, you know.
Heck, I wouldn't do this for *anyone* else.
I baked bread for you.
Bread.
Me.
I was actually standing there in the kitchen, up to my elbows in flour, dough digging under my fingernails, because I know how you feel about fresh-baked bread on the table.

And did I tell you that the phone rang?
Yeah. And because I was expecting a call, I went digging through my bag with powdery hands, so my stuff was left covered with smudges from the flour, from the dough for the bread that I wouldn't be making for anybody else.

So I hope you appreciate the effort.
Because I don't do this for just anybody.
—Me.

The Sabbath bee

All day I have been traveling from flower to flower, distracted by every bright color under the sun. Now as darkness falls I lay down my burdens, the collected pollen of a day's work, and I give myself over to a welcoming family and the sweetness of rest.

No briefcase

Shabbat does not come in with the clink of polished black loafers. He does not settle his briefcase or his laptop case on the floor. He doesn't even own a wallet.

Shabbat isn't stressed out, doesn't bring the office home with him. He doesn't tell the kids to leave him alone for a few minutes while he unwinds.

It's easy for Shabbat, because he doesn't *have* an office. His workweek consists of sitting at a table with friends, with wine and good food. Shabbat comes in after the errands are done, when the table is set and everything is out of the oven.

Still, after Shabbat settles in he's so likeable that it's hard to be frustrated with his happy-go-lucky lifestyle. And I *do* keep inviting him back. The weekend wouldn't be the same without him.

Dancing shoes

These shoes? I've had them for years. They're really good shoes, comfortable—the kind that you can wear your whole life so long as you take care of them. Every week before I put them on I look them over, polish them up, but besides normal wear and tear they don't need much maintenance. The stitching is strong, and the leather is still in great condition even after all this time.

Obviously I don't wear them on the street or every day—they're dancing shoes, after all. They need smooth wood surfaces. The grit and gravel would ruin them. They're made for a specific purpose.

And just so you know, when the music starts and I slip them on, sometimes I feel like I'm flying.

Pet shop with allegory

Shabbat tells the story of the time when she went to the pet store. There was a box full of adorable tiny puppies, but she could only pick one. The puppies all ran away from her—except for one little runt with floppy ears. And Shabbat picked up that puppy and she said, "I will love you and feed you and take you on walks, so long as you play with me and welcome me home every day." So Shabbat and the puppy lived happily ever after.

"A puppy?" I ask when she finishes. "Really? In your version I'm a *puppy?*"

"Yeah, why not? Just look at those big brown eyes. You are *so cute!*"

Before I can stop her, Shabbat leans over and ruffles my hair. I protest, but I know that if that's how she remembers the story, then that's how the story's getting told.

Double manna

In olden times, when food from skies was the only way to dine,
And the Sabbath's rest was ensured and blessed by Friday morning time,
With manna once and manna twice, double providence divine,
Our stomachs filled with heaven's yield, headier than wine.

Big and small

I believe in the relevance of this nightfall when I stand in the prairie, under a round sky deeper than eternity, colder and more distant than the human mind can bear.

I believe in the significance of Shabbat, though the urban skyline pushes me in, and the only stars are the ones that circle above, waiting for permission to land.

I wrap myself, my family, my life in Shabbat because it holds back the agoraphobic world, pulls in horizons and levels the sprawling towers. In another day they will spill out uncontrolled, but for tonight the world is made up of only a handful of people and enough time to enjoy their presence.

Invisible royalty

Because Shabbat has no physical form, it instead imposes reality upon the pre-existing world around it. It smooths over rough walkways, adding a sheen and a softness to cement and filling out the missing branches of storm-damaged trees.

This improved world is only visible to those whose hearts beat in time to Shabbat's singular destiny. Their neighbors must think it odd see otherwise rather sane individuals carefully pulling off coats and gloves as though they were made of ermine and velvet, and raising plastic cups of juice in tribute as they would goblets of gold-flecked ambrosia or sparkling champagne in the hall of the king.

Clubhouse

"We built our clubhouse together, the two of us. I painted and found some old furniture and made it look nice, but I don't know nothing about construction. If I had made it by myself, the roof would leak and there would still be holes in the walls near the ground."

"Sure, I did the patching and the roofwork—but it would have been a pretty pathetic place to hang out without all your work to make it feel like home."

"Oh—but don't forget Mom and Dad! It was Dad who let us use his old shed and paid for new materials. Otherwise we wouldn't have this place at all. And probably we wouldn't have worked so hard if Mom didn't make snacks and always say what a good job we were doing."

"So it was a team effort, huh? No one could have made this great clubhouse alone."

Blind date

There are a thousand things I could be doing right now. Exciting things. Necessary things. But, no. A mutual friend foisted Shabbat on me. Because I owe this guy big I put on a strained smile and said, "Great. I love hanging out with Shabbat!"

I sit across the table from Shabbat, making polite conversation and watching the clock.

Just twenty-three more hours, and I'm free. Twenty-two more hours. Twenty-one....

Just be

All Sunday long, I do errands.
Monday I do the weekday grind.
Tuesday I do the emergencies that pop up from every corner.
I do the slow march toward the weekend, starting sometime Wednesday afternoon.
Thursday—time to do the shopping, do the menu planning, do what prep work I can.
So that Friday I can do those last few chores, trying to do everything on time.

Shabbat. I stop, I listen, and I take the time to be.

Grandpa's house

I can't wait to go to Grandpa's house! I've been looking forward to it forever. We'll get out of the car, and he'll be waiting on the porch for us. He'll give me a giant hug, and he'll say, "Look how big you are! You've been eating your vegetables!" And, and, I'll go inside and sit in the sagging green chair, and eat cashews from the candy bowl and Grandpa will let me have some coffee in my milk, and we'll hear the latest news about the neighborhood, look at pictures and tell stories about things that happened before I was born!

Dad smiles. "But that's what happens every time we visit. Shouldn't we try something new?"

No way! That's how visiting Grandpa *goes*. If we changed something, it just wouldn't be the same.

Creeping sunlight

I sit reading under a wide-leafed tree on a late summer afternoon. The hours must have tiptoed past, because golden-yellow Shabbat has sneaked up behind me, crawling close on flaxen fingers.

The cicadas hum a restful melody, and the red-winged blackbirds know all the right songs to greet the rising dusk.

Four somethings

Shabbat is…

…as old as the shift from day to night, the desire for rest after hard work.

…newer than today's dawn, and fresher than this morning's dew.

…borrowed time from the world to come, a dip into eternity.

…that shade of dark, poignant blue that comes to the sky after sunset, before pure night. The color so thick with tones and subtleties that it almost hurts to watch it change into black.

Came for me

I didn't expect Shabbat to come looking for me. Usually I'm the one trying to peek over all the heads in the room, wondering when *he'll* arrive. This week I didn't want to bother with the crowds. I went straight home, opened the door. Stepped inside—and there he was.

Fire in his eyes, hair oiled back, and—was that cologne? "You came to *me*," I said quietly, unaccountably pleased.

He didn't answer, but instead stepped forward until I was pressed against the closed door. We were so close that the tips of our noses brushed. I tried to recognize the scent he was wearing.

The kisses of his mouth were warmer than the summer evening.

Blanket

Shabbat is a blanket large enough to cover my head and drop all the way over my feet. It is thick enough to block everything out, and comfortable enough to provide me with the best nap of my life.

Closets

Shabbat has deep, dark closets lining its hallway, dank from tears and peopled with a cemetery's worth of moldy skeletons.

Shabbat's closets are formidable, but so are the thick hardwood doors that close them, the iron locks that twist shut with a dry clang.

And carved on the doors in thick gothic letters are the words, "Do not open until Saturday, after dark."

To the Choirmaster: A solo for violin

(Shabbat Nachamu)

Holy is the empty space, the void within form.

When we are pulled taut by the extremes of life, by conflicting desires, when we tremble in the guideless air, isolated even from those who are closest to us,

Holy is the gaping dark.

Though we are powerless before the rod, caught within our own chafing limitations, the forces that press and move us—nevertheless,

Holy is the unknowable abyss below.

Because in the clear still night, when we cry into the holes in the center of our being, our voices will echo in the place where there is nothing, and out will pour a song of comfort, clean and pure and soothing against the black.

Storm

Where does the storm come from? What ends with lightning and thunder begins with the twin wings of a butterfly, magnesium blue, flickering and fluttering across the dreams of creation.

It might take a while for the sky to open, but from that first wing-beat the storm is inevitable. Pressure eases, clouds begin to gather, and a warm wind blows.

Evaporation, condensation, precipitation. The cycle began long before humans. Before monkeys, before birds or even plants. It is a part of our world, ecologically ordained. When the air changes though, it affects something primal within every living thing. We look to the sky. We wait for the rain.

The bride

A white leather pump splashes through a puddle on the curb but continues on its frenzied way. The light is red, but the woman in the full-skirted wedding dress runs across, her arms full of white ruffles and tulle. Cars screech to a halt, taxis honk as she glances briefly at them, but she can't stop. Everyone is expecting her.

The Sabbath bride throws open the double doors at the back of the synagogue just as the people rise to their feet. Her chest is heaving and her hair has come loose to fall in curls around her face. Her cheeks are red from exertion but she can't help smiling at the exhilarating feeling that she gets every time a room full of people turns to welcome her home.

Letter

The letter arrived halfway through the week. On heavy cardstock, *You know I'm coming. Be ready.*

I sighed and tucked it into my pocket. The reminder really hadn't been necessary.

The luckiest person

"I had so many calls to make at work today—but just when I thought I would go crazy, Shabbat told me to go home and said he'd take care of the rest."

"Really? I was at the end of a long checkout line with just one item, and Shabbat let me go ahead of him."

"Shabbat gave me his seat on the subway when I was so tired that I thought I would fall over."

"This Shabbat sounds like the same guy who cleared my sidewalk along with his own after the last snowstorm. What an amazing guy! I wonder if he's seeing anyone."

"When he opened the door for me yesterday, I noticed a wedding ring. Man, what I wouldn't give for a guy like that!"

I glance down at the band on my finger and hide a smile. He's a catch, all right.

Water damage

Sometimes life slams into you like raging floodwaters, ripping up your most carefully laid plans and clearing away the collected dust and debris of the years.

Sometimes life seeps in, boring subtly through the hidden cracks to drip questions and new growth into your unsuspecting world.

That might be why Shabbat sometimes appears slowly, like a gathering of gray clouds on the far horizon, and sometimes with the immediacy of a lightning bolt ripping through the retaining walls.

Beads
(Rosh Hashanah)

Shabbat clinks into place with the lacquered clarity of a bead sliding onto a necklace string. At this stage, the new Shabbat is clear and unmarked—a perfect pearl.

It takes its place along the length with nearly a year's worth of Shabbats, each one engraved with the faces of all the people I saw that day. The workmanship is flawless.

Soon this bead too will grow heavy with the gilt edges of delicate designs, dozens of tiny faces etched upon its surface.

The necklace weighs down like a yoke upon my shoulders, almost choking me.

Is it heavier than usual, or do I simply notice the weight because I know that the jeweler will be coming soon, to examine each individual bead and determine the value of my year?

Combat nurse
(*Shabbat Shuvah*)

The siege ended two days ago. Now is a time of respite and negotiation. The battered and injured are still, gathering their strength in this quiet time between battles.

I see Shabbat approaching, but she is no longer my well-heeled, festive beloved. She has laid aside her glittering gown for a plain white smock, tucked her hair under a kerchief and scrubbed her face clean of makeup. She pauses beside each soul, offering rest and comfort to those who quake at the prospect of the coming struggle. Her feet slap softly against the rough floor as she approaches me.

"Take courage," she whispers, lifting medicinal wine to my lips. As she presses a crust of bread to my palm, her smile offers a promise of sweet times yet to come. She moves to her next patient, and I realize that she has never been more beautiful.

Not white
(Yom Kippur)

Yom Kippur's robes are the color of light that has never fractured. Unadulterated, all-encompassing, streaming, shining *white*. Yom Kippur wears the white of the sun, of angels and the holiest consecrated secrets. Watching it too long is to risk earthly blindness, to willingly wither away.

There are millions of colors in Shabbat's coat—a rainbow in every fold. Yellow-brown, ruby-black, rust-gold, cream-peach and more blues than there are permutations in the sea.

Shabbat does not wear Yom Kippur white, though. Every thread in Shabbat's coat is a remnant of shattered perfection—a soothing multi-faced retelling of the cornea-burning whiteness.

Yom Kippur is draped in purity. Shabbat's sleeves are lined with loam-brown and blood-red, edged with silver-embroidered teardrops.

I wear Shabbat's coat because it matches the world I walk through. It looks like peace and restlessness, compassion and gloating, spring, autumn and dawn. It is cut to human size.

Nothing new
(Sukkot)

Week after week Shabbat comes in, Shabbat goes out. The Earth rotates without end. So long as twilight gives way to dawn, there will be one day in seven when Shabbat can slip into the world.

For those who live by that seventh day, Shabbat is a constant. An eternal connection. Generations pass away, new ones arise, and the same songs lift to the same sky from different mouths. The young become old and new feet take on the inexorable march to death, but Shabbat does not change. If the short-lived people who look to the sky invite Shabbat again to their table, Shabbat will come. Until the sun goes out and Earth ceases its circling.

(…And even then, if our descendants escape before the end they will probably find a way to take Shabbat to other worlds.)

The sleepy guest

I arrive home from work to find Shabbat asleep on the couch, one bare foot dangling over the edge. I put down my things and creep into the room as quietly as I can.

Shabbat's eyes open, bleary but content. "Welcome back," Shabbat murmurs sleepily, burrowing deeper into the cushions.

"Welcome back yourself," I say, crouching near the floor so I can look at Shabbat face-to-half-awake-face. "We're not going out tonight, are we?"

"I baked cookies," Shabbat says, and I notice that the room does smell of sugar and chocolate and childhood. "Let me sleep some more, and maybe we can hang out later. Okay?"

I lean forward and kiss Shabbat on the nose. "That sounds perfect," I say.

Becomes easy

The first moment of Shabbat is when everything becomes easy.

Shabbat is the waterslide after waiting in line under the summer sun. Shabbat is the tiny change in calculation that makes X finally mark the spot. It is the moment when the 3-D picture resolves itself, when the pie dough reaches the right consistency. Shabbat is slippers after stilettos, a real hug after a week of quick pats on the back. When the curtains open and the first streams of Shabbat shine in, the middling details and distant humming vanish.

It all happens in the flare of a match, the last sliver of sunlight. You just have to know the magic words.

Looked everywhere

I was looking for you on Tuesday, even though I knew you weren't coming until Friday. There was this glittering, perfect moment, and it felt like you were near. Then Wednesday night, out drinking with friends, I felt carefree in a way that made me turn around, *sure* that you were somewhere in the room.

By Friday night I could hardly wait. I craned my neck every time someone approached, and when I finally saw you coming toward me I rushed to meet you.

Just cuddle

Battered by the week, I lean into Shabbat. "Can we just cuddle tonight?"

Time change

Shabbat scrambles in on polished Mary Janes, rushing across the room to where I sit at my desk. "I'm here!" she announces, her arms thrust wide.

I keep writing.

Shabbat grabs my pen, throwing it across the room.

"Hey, I was using that!" I snap.

"But I'm *here*!"

I glance at my watch. "Well, you shouldn't be. It's only 4:30."

Shabbat folds her arms. "But I'm *here*."

I sigh. "I see that you are. So, how do you want to spend all this extra time?"

Shabbat stares at her feet. "Um…"

I resist the urge to groan. "You're here an hour early, and you don't have a plan?"

"That's your job!" Shabbat yells, stomping one tiny foot. Then she collapses on the floor, red folds of skirt fanning out around her.

I settle beside her, wrapping my arms around her tiny shoulders. It's going to be one of those evenings.

Guerilla performance art

Shabbat came like guerilla performance art, like a carefully orchestrated act that began so subtly that few pedestrians even noticed until it was underway. The streets were full, and everyone *seemed* to be doing their own thing, but then at some secret sign they came together for a shared purpose. It wasn't destructive, not particularly helpful—it just was. The observers, the people who hadn't been involved in the act, shrugged and went on to their next errands.

Nights like this

On clear nights like this, when the glimmers of tiny distant suns sparkle pristinely in the firmament above,

When the rotation of our orbiting world has brought forth the evening, and the heavens proclaim the glory of God,

On nights like this, when all the children of Abraham are represented upon a cloudless canvas,

And the moon is nearly overflowing with light,

The frozen sky would still feel lonely,

If I didn't have you to share it with.

Winter wonderland

Shabbat has strong features, dark hair, and he is wearing a tuxedo when he beckons me from the other side of the curtain.

I join him in a tent made of silver, walls arching toward the sky and frost-kissed branches tangling overhead. I am suddenly wearing a silver-sequined gown, glittering in the light of a thousand candles shining two by two in the periphery.

Shabbat settles a firm hand beneath my shoulder, and as the music starts we sweep into the crisp stillness of the early winter sunset.

Stopping by the bookstore on a snowy evening

(Just to browse for a while, because I'm already keeping one of the most important promises I've ever made, and I don't have far to walk before I get to curl up under my comforter and sleep uninterrupted through the cold, still night.)

Pockets of delight

And when God had finished all of God's work, mankind took charge. The wonders of creation were replaced by the assembly-line precision of resentful accuracy. Mindless hammer blows beat swords into plowshares, then back into swords, depending upon which was more fashionable at the time. And work never ceased, from one day to the next.

But there are pockets of delight to be found, moments and places of fellowship where one unique and beautiful human speaks to another, where worth is measured by kindness and where the sparkle in a loved one's eyes is worth more than diamonds.

Holiday guests
(*Hanukkah*)

This week, Shabbat is babysitting.

"I'm the youngest of seven," she says, "and sometimes I miss all the activity of a full house."

She's pulled out all the stops, bringing in heaps of toys and candy to keep everyone happy. When her eight fiery-haired nephews come spilling in through the front door, Shabbat instantly shifts from the perfect hostess to "the cool aunt." It doesn't seem to bother her that she's about to have a house full of rambunctious troublemakers all hyped up on sugar.

"Let them have their fun," she says when the youngest splatters olive oil across the tablecloth and the rug. "I barely ever get to see them. I want to make sure they enjoy their visit."

Winter white

Shabbat stopped in front of me when I was hurrying along the sidewalk. "Why the rush?" she asked, wrapping her thickly robed arms around me.

The wind was slicing though the wool and cotton that I wore in layers, but the fluffy softness of Shabbat's wrap kept out every hint of winter. Shabbat's fingertips glowed and were almost hot as they meandered gently up my arm.

I fell asleep in a thick warm haze.

Tropical paradise

I dressed for winter before stepping outside to pick up Shabbat. He was waiting by the bus stop, holding an overnight bag and wearing a bright, almost glowing Hawaiian shirt.

"Aren't you cold?" I called as I walked toward him. His tanned brown skin, open to the elements, clashed with my thick, water-resistant coat.

"'*Cold*'?" He stretched out his arms. "Are you kidding me? Baby, I'm sunshine and mai tais 24/7!"

I frowned down at the gray, packed-frost sidewalk. "Are those *orchids* growing out of the cement?" I demanded, pointing at a short trail from the curb to his sandaled feet.

Instead of answering, Shabbat wrapped his arms around me. He smelled like coconut with a soft tang of seawater. I wanted to ask him what kept his skin so warm, but as soon as I opened my mouth he smothered me with his tropical optimism.

The cover of night

Night falls, the darkness spreading over the sky as a shelter of peace. On Shabbat someone asks, "To what can the black sky be likened?"

One says—to the roof of a tent.

(But no, a tent protects from storms and poor weather, while the night sky often brings with it rain or hail.)

Says another—to a covering blanket. (But although Shabbat is a day of rest, surely most celebrants will be awake very late, enjoying its festive cheer.)

Is not the darkness of Shabbat like a wedding canopy? asks a third.

(Perhaps, but only two stand beneath a wedding canopy, while the whole world is shadowed by the dark.)

And finally a child speaks, saying, "The sky of Shabbat is like dress-up clothes, that let anyone underneath become a king or queen for just a little while."

Snowflakes

Each human being is as unique as a carefully crafted snowflake, as breakable and fragile as a tiny shard of frosty rococo.

Shabbat remains as faithful and unmoving as stone.

Those drawn to Shabbat come in gusts and flurries, soon to be gathered and tightly packed.

The sky darkens. The snow deepens, swirling and eddying upon a frozen mountaintop. Uniqueness piles upon uniqueness, pressing together, unifying beneath a thick, churning storm.

Snow falls week after week.

If enough snowflakes gather, the mountaintop will hum and vibrate—

And all the collected drifts will surge together into the valley below.

In a single word: בדיבור אחד

Come home early from work. Dance under the stars at midnight. Eat ice cream. Watch a movie. Play hide and seek with the cousins. Laugh until your ribs hurt. Go to synagogue. Play with the cat. Sleep and sleep and sleep some more.

They all sound so different, but when I listen to what everyone is doing tonight, I only hear one word, really.

Shabbat.

Fairy tale

Once upon a time, a farmer stumbled into an underground bower where a fairy of astonishing beauty begged him to cease plowing the land just above her home, lest he tear through her packed-earth ceiling. In return for protecting her and voluntarily lessening his crop yield, she plied him with platters of fruit, bright as jewels, and a bowl of nectar gathered from midnight-blooming flowers.

The clever storyteller will say that the farmer is the Jewish people and the fairy is Shabbat, providing immeasurable reward for a day's leisure.

(But I see Shabbat in the bowl of honeyed nectar, warm as a midsummer evening and smelling of lavender, primrose and jasmine. Surely the bowl must remain full to the brim no matter how many mouthfuls the greedy farmer drinks, as his fields, his work, and all sense of time slip away, replaced with giddy satisfaction.)

On Shabbat

My friend came early, letting herself in through the front door and running into the living room on wobbly legs.

"Hi there," I greeted her just before she pounced.

"It's so great to see you!" She wrapped her arms around me, almost chokingly tight. "It's been *forever*! Is that a new shirt? It looks *great* on you. Gorgeous. That color really works. Is that water you're drinking? Can I have some?"

She grabbed my glass and drank. "Hey, this is *good water*! I *love* it! Where did you get it?"

"The… tap?" I watched her savor it like fine wine. "Sweetie, are you okay?"

"I feel fabulous!" She kicked her feet into the air, toes wriggling, as she giggled.

Finally, I couldn't take it any more. "What are you *on* tonight?" I demanded.

"Shabbat!" she announced, falling on the couch and laughing like she would never stop.

Pity date

When I come running in—late, frazzled, tossed together—you are already there. Everyone is gathered around you, and you look *good*. You probably spent the whole week choosing just the right everything, while I was keeping appointments and rushing to catch up and losing sleep over every workaday disaster.

Now though, my shoes are scuffed and considering how I rushed to get here I'm lucky if my buttons are even aligned. If anyone saw the two of us together they'd probably assume you were on a pity date. I blush and hang back, letting you flirt with your gaggle of well-wishers.

But then a hand touches my lower back and there you are! "It's so good to see you," you whisper in my ear, words that I know you mean only for me.

Above the tablecloth

Tonight, I've invited Shabbat to come home with me.

I tried to act casual about it, but I can barely contain my excitement. I've laid out a freshly-laundered cloth, smoothed it over the surface of the table and covered it with laden bowls and platters. I meet Shabbat over the tabletop and we make small talk. We speak casually, as if we don't know where the night will take us. Shabbat notices the ambiance of candleglow, and I know that Shabbat has been waiting all week for this meeting.

Music rises softly—nearby, someone is serenading my guest.

The tablecloth is rumpled. Plates tumble and crash to the floor. Sated and exhausted, I pour more wine as words tumble from my mouth.

Sunday's child

Sunday's child knows what's coming,
Monday's child starts the week running.
Tuesday's child is tied up in knots,
While Wednesday's on schedule but sort of forgot
That Thursday's needs help with a major display
That's in shambles and can't be put off 'til Friday—

While the Sabbath's child (it would be understood)
Is blithe and bonny, gay and good.
He's the king of the couplets, the crown of the rhyme,
The nursery's champion; a child sublime.
He is always well-mannered, cheerful and meek,
For he dumps all his flaws on the rest of the week.

Cause and effect

Shabbat called me Friday morning. "I'm looking forward to seeing you tonight. You have something planned, right?"

"Wha—I—of course. *Of course* I have something planned, Shabbat. Why would you even ask?" I looked guiltily around the room, hoping no one would catch me in the lie.

I was feeling a little annoyed as I scanned my contacts, trying to think of *anyone* who might be free, who would be willing to get together for a last-minute shindig.

That night, after a great meal and in the middle of a lively conversation, Shabbat leaned over to murmur in my ear. "You're welcome."

"For what?"

Shabbat gestured around the room.

I frowned. "You think I'm thankful to *you* for the party that *I* put together for *your* benefit?"

The look Shabbat gave me was a little pitying. "Seriously. What would you be doing tonight if it weren't for me?"

The Sabbath tree

One Sunday, when I was small, I took the bag of havdalah spices and buried it in the back yard. The sun shone down on the spot, and I watered it daily. A tiny stem sprouted, with silken-green leaves, and every day it grew more. By Friday morning it was a sapling taller than I was, with tight buds at the end of its branches. Through the day I checked on it, watching the buds slowly open.

As the sun set, the smell of spices seemed to fill the air. Just as darkness crept into the yard, the flowers opened wide. They had white, glowing petals that curved like shaved cinnamon, with tiny star anise-shaped patterns within. I sat under the tree all evening and much of the next day, breathing in cardamom and turmeric until the sky darkened again and the petals snowed slowly down.

Haiku

If the collected knowledge of the world were condensed into a single haiku,
    Shabbat would be the fleeting and pleasant sound
    Of the brush stroking the parchment.

If all eternity were lived in the span of a single day,
    Then the magical, liminal moments of dawn and dusk
    Would be the eras of Shabbat.

When a table is set with every delicious treat of nature,
    Then Shabbat is present
    In the laughter and conversation of the diners.

And if all love were collected in a single heart,
    One would find Shabbat in the curve of the arm, the sound of the voice,
    That significant detail that means "you" to me.

Lifeblood

They all entered into the flow, constricted by the walls but refreshed, red with excitement and propelled forward by a force they could not control.

They came trudging in at the end of the cycle, fatigued and stumbling along, demanding replenishment, needing energy before they could do it all again—

And then they joined together, pulled by an irresistible desire—and with an uprising of might they crushed through, crossed the barrier into a new realm—which was the same realm they had entered thousands of times before.

Past the electric, frenetic crush, the sweetest part came—when they entered the red-walled chamber, the treasure-room where fresh air and new energy were freely given to all. They lingered for a moment, luxuriating, before they began the cycle again.

Hiddur mitzvah

So this Wednesday in Hebrew school we learned about *hiddur mitzvah*—that's making all your Jewish stuff look as pretty as you can because it shows God how much you like being Jewish and making God happy. And anyway, so I decorated my very own *shabbos* candlesticks, with gemstones and yellow paint, and I worked really hard at it, and at the end of class my teacher smiled and said, "Good job!"

Last night Friday, while Daddy was driving home he stopped at the light on top of the hill, and after he stopped Mommy said, "Look at that sunset!" And then we all looked, and it was bright pink and my favorite color orange with just a little bit of sun halfway set, and the clouds looked like carnival cotton candy.

Then the light turned green and Daddy kept driving and I whispered to God, "Good job!"

Flower bride

Stitch lavender into your hems, my dear, the purple buds like the first dark corners of evening, the smell of comfort and treasures lovingly, safely packed away.

Weave anemones through the fringes of your gown. Mix dark and light in single broad flourishes.

Teach the sweet peas, with their smell of clean and open spaces, to grow along your train.

Tuck lilies of the valley into your hair my love, and clip gardenias around your ankles so that their rich, noble fragrance will follow your footsteps.

May you be sated with delicacies of candied pansies and roses, to bring deep red to your lips and pink to your cheeks, purple to color the irises of your eyes and palest white to your fingertips.

And meet me in the garden at nightfall, under the wisteria canopy.

Exact timing

I wanted to know the precise moment when Shabbat came. I wanted to see the shift, from week to -end, work to rest. They told me that Shabbat came with the sunset, was born in shadows, and so I sat and waited on a high peak. Behind me, the sinking sun. Before me, the stretching shadows.

And as the blush turned to gray and the shadows grew quiet, the wind laughed. "You could have called me. I was waiting, and it would have saved you some time."

"I didn't see you come in," I whispered, sorry that I had failed.

"You must have blinked," the wind replied, blowing past me and into Shabbat.

Macaroni necklace

It was a macaroni necklace day. A seat of your pants, *I saw this thirty seconds ago in a shop window and it sorta reminded me of you*, I can't find my glasses—you mean the ones you're wearing right now?—sort of a day.

I should probably be embarrassed. I made tea sandwiches for the queen of the week and left the crusts on. I nodded off in the corner and slept through the entire grand fanfare, trumpets and all.

But Shabbat didn't say anything. In fact, I may have just dreamed it, but I'd swear she pulled her foot out of her diamond-studded heel at one point to show me the run in her stocking, one toe poking out, before she tucked her foot back in her shoe and let a boisterous gang of children lead her onto the dance floor.

Pomegranate

Shabbat is in my kitchen late Friday afternoon, standing beside the fruit bowl and examining a dark, round pomegranate. "What is this?" he asks.

So I tell him that the pomegranate is one of the seven species, that its profile was stitched on the hems of the high priests' robes. I mention that the rabbis claimed that it has 613 seeds inside, one for every commandment.

"Really?" Shabbat tries to smell the odorless fruit. Then he perks up and presses his nails through the thick outer skin, splitting it down the middle. He looks carefully inside, as though counting every seed, and then he shrugs and hands me half. With cherry-stained fingers, he pulls out a clump of seeds and stuffs it in his mouth like a greedy child. "You forgot to mention that they're tangy and sweet… and crunchy," he reproaches me, his mouth still full.

Wardrobe choice

I can imagine Shabbat standing in her walk-in closet this afternoon. She probably pulled out the rainbow mini-dress first, the one with every color imaginable splashed across it, like an iridescent—and very fashionable—Jackson Pollock canvas stitched into a shape that hugged all her curves.

And then the basic, backless midnight-blue sheath, made from silk woven from the first dreams of bedtime. A simple and elegant, admiring "wow" of a dress, as opposed to the eye-catching, elaborate painted extravaganza.

In the end she put on the colorful one, along with striped tights and clunky, candy-colored bangles, peacock feathers in her hair and makeup straight from the eighties. Don't get me wrong; she pulled it off marvelously. Still, I do wish she had worn the simpler dress tonight.

Or, alternately, just something from the lingerie drawer.

Quiet spaces

Shabbat loves the quiet spaces, you know.

Sure, you expect to see him in big, boisterous rooms filled with laugher and singing, sitting at tables warping under the weight of good food, writing guest lists a mile long that keep growing with every somebody who looks a little lonely on the way home.

But Shabbat also likes the quiet spaces.

He likes big, yawning chambers, with maybe two or three people talking earnestly in the corner. He likes simple companionship, the silence between good friends. Shabbat values quality above quantity. He would rather have all your dreams than everyone's favorite movies.

When you see him laughing in a crowded room, you might notice that he's not always all there. He likes the bluster and the mirth—

But he *loves* the quiet spaces.

The art of a perfect sunset

Shabbat was already on the patio when we walked outside to eat. He wasn't dressed for a summer dinner, though. He wore overalls splattered with glittering, iridescent paint—colors that could have come straight from another world.

"Dinner entertainment," Shabbat said, guessing our question. "Don't mind me. Just sit down and enjoy your meal."

And then he dipped a paintbrush into the carrots. He lifted it with a blob of orange at its tip toward the washed-out blue-white sky, and he applied the color just below some wispy clouds. He did the same with the cranberry glaze and the curried lentils, and then he splattered some wine on the eastern horizon, letting it seep through and darken his canvas.

He kept working through dinner and dessert, until the time came to roll coffee over the sky and scatter handfuls of sugar crystals across it to sweeten the darkness.

A song for Shabbat

Shabbat she sits, staring—seeming to stir when I start to sing but only swaying softly, her starlit eyes conspicuously somber as she searches across the scattered landscape. Does she seem scared? I yearn to assuage her fears, to assure her even in her unsettled stupor that she is the sole possessor of my spiritual devotion, that if she should smile—only smile!—my soul would shatter into shards and wisps of splendor.

Road ends

Shabbat? It's a lot like driving forty miles over the speed limit when all of a sudden a sign in front of you announces, "Road ends, 500 feet," and sure enough, 500 feet later there's no road and you have to smear rubber across the highway because otherwise you'll drive into thin air. You're in a hurry and there are places you have to be but the road just *isn't there* right now, though the workmen tell you to be patient because it'll be up again soon… -ish.

You can get mad, sure, you can yell or make frustrated phone calls and pace, but instead maybe you pocket your keys and step outside. There's a field of wildflowers in the median and the birds are singing, and even though you'll have to work twice as hard to catch up, you don't mind the delay—not really.

Reluctant Shabbat

Shabbat was hiding.

Somewhere in the house, I hoped. The windows were all closed, and anyway I hated the idea of him lost in the hard, unfriendly outside. I looked everywhere, pretending that I was just cleaning as I checked under the couch, behind the curtains, in drawers.

No luck. Next I tried to lure him with the smell of pie just out of the oven, fresh bread from the bakery. Nothing.

I lit candles hoping to attract him like a moth. I sang his favorite songs.

Finally, I gave up. I collapsed on the sofa and watched the candles burn until the room went dark.

…And sometime in the middle of the night I woke up with a crick in my neck and the warm, fuzzy feeling of Shabbat curled up warm against my stomach. I shifted to a more comfortable position and fell back asleep.

Stayed the night

I yawn and stretch, my toes wriggling out past the bottom of the sheets.

My arm brushes against bare skin. Yep, there's Shabbat lying beside me, fast asleep.

He started staying the night recently, and there's nothing unusual about waking up beside him.

It feels nice, having him there.

Memory lane

Shabbat plopped down beside me on the couch, holding an open photo album. He pointed to a picture of the two of us sitting together on a park bench. "Remember our first date?" he asked.

"'First date'?" I snatched the album away and flipped back a few pages. "We'd been going out for almost a year by then."

"Were we? You weren't that into me in the beginning," Shabbat said frankly. "You were always ditching me for anyone more interesting. Not taking me seriously."

"Well, you *were* really high-maintenance. Not to mention freakishly commitment-oriented."

"So I have high expectations. I'm not *so* hard to live with, am I?"

Before I could really get the fight going, I noticed a picture of one of our more sublime evenings. "You're an acquired taste," I conceded. And quietly enough that he wouldn't hear, "Acquired and addictive."

Weekday ruins
(Tu Bishvat)

The sun sets on the city where people once toiled. Darkness falls over stone structures, walls crumble to ruins.

The piles of stone are given time to grow.

Rain falls, the sun shines, and green shoots peek through the cracks on a once flawless façade.

When human labor ceases, the earth returns to its original state. The garden creeps in from the edges, and with every day of rest the Tree of Life lowers its branches nearer to the ground.

Too far

I lit every candle in the house, hours before sunset. You probably felt like I was holding my finger down on your doorbell, or yelling up at you from the courtyard. I don't know if you thought it was endearing and cute or really f-ing annoying.

It's hard to tell with you sometimes, and I don't always think it's fair. You demand so much of me that I sometimes wonder if I'm losing myself in you, but if I do lose track of *me* in the day-long spans of *you*, then there you are shaking your head and muttering that I don't get it at all. But the second I do something you don't like, you let me know. Boy, do you ever let me know.

If I tried too hard this time, then I hope you don't mind. I just wanted to make you smile.

Havdalah

Shabbat is a single flame, shining through our interwoven lives. Shabbat grows in intensity every time another soul joins her tapestry, dancing and growing until it seems that her light will illumine every dark place. The flame expands and brightens, overtaking the world of darkness until—suddenly—it goes out.

Water balloons
(Shabbat Zakhor)

I was walking down the sidewalk, my mind on other things, when a water balloon splashed onto the ground in front of me.

"Hey!" I yelled, jumping back too late to keep my feet dry. From an upstairs window, two freckled, gap-toothed faces grinned down at me. "Purim, cut it out!" I yelled, glaring at the younger child.

"It was her," Purim said, pointing at his partner in crime. Shabbat nodded, grinning wickedly.

"I think I can guess who came up with the idea," I muttered, right before another water balloon hit the crown of my head.

"All right, three-pointer!" Purim announced. I wiped water off my face and looked up just in time to see them exchange high fives. Purim handed Shabbat another full balloon, and I started running.

www.ingramcontent.com/pod-product-compliance
Lightning Source LLC
LaVergne TN
LVHW041343080426
835512LV00006B/598